Butterfly

Nancy Dickmann

BROWN BEAR BOOKS

Published by Brown Bear Books Ltd
4877 N. Circulo Bujia
Tucson, AZ 85718
USA

and

Unit 1/D, Leroy House
436 Essex Rd
London N1 3QP
UK

ISBN 978-1-78121-535-7 (library bound)
ISBN 978-1-78121-562-3 (paperback)

Library of Congress Cataloging-in-Publication Data available on request

Text: Nancy Dickmann
Design Manager: Keith Davis
Picture Manager: Sophie Mortimer
Children's Publisher: Anne O'Daly

Manufactured in the United States of America
CPSIA compliance information: Batch#AG/5633

Picture Credits
The photographs in this book are used by permission and through the courtesy of:

Cover: Shutterstock: Ron Rowan Photography cl, Kate Scott main, Smidthy West bl, Rafael Viralalta tl; Interior: Dreamstime: Amanda Melones 12–13; iStock: aliblec 4–5, dossyl 13, 14, 20bc, Helene H 11, JHVE Photo 18–19, Jay Ondreicka 10–11, 20br, SolStock 14–15; Public Domain: wisc.edu/curbarchive/Tamya Hall 16–17; Shutterstock: Kate Besler 21, Arto Hakola 4, Edmund Neo 17, Isabelle Ohara 16, Jay Ondreicka 8, Sari ONeal 6, 6–7, 8–9, 20tl, 20tr, Jane Zalewski 1, 18, 20bl.

All other artwork and photography © Brown Bear Books.

t-top, r-right, l-left, c-center, b-bottom

Brown Bear Books has made every attempt to contact the copyright holder. If you have any information about omissions please contact: licensing@brownbearbooks.co.uk

Websites
The website addresses in this book were valid at the time of going to press. However, it is possible that contents or addresses may change following publication of this book. No responsibility for any such changes can be accepted by the author or the publisher. Readers should be supervised when they access the Internet.

Words in **bold** appear in the Useful Words on page 23.

Contents

What Is a Life Cycle?

All living things have a life cycle.
A mother has babies. The babies grow up.
As adults, they have babies of their own.
The mother dies, but her family lives on.

Some baby insects look very different from their parents. This is a baby ladybug!

Butterflies are insects. Many insects have an unusual life cycle. They are born looking one way. But partway through their lives, they change. Butterflies follow this life cycle.

It Starts With an Egg

A monarch butterfly lays a single egg. She lays it on a leaf. The egg is the size of a pinhead. It will be about four days before it hatches.

The caterpillar inside can be seen through the thin eggshell.

A tiny caterpillar crawls out. It is white, with a black head. It looks nothing like the butterfly that laid the egg. For its first meal, it eats the empty eggshell.

WOW!

Some insects lay lots of eggs. An African driver ant can produce millions of eggs.

Caterpillars

The young stage of an insect's life is a **larva**.
The caterpillar is a larva. It has no wings.
Its body is divided into three parts.

Birds eat caterpillars.
Disguise helps some caterpillars stay safe.
Some have spots that look like eyes.

The larva has six pairs of eyes. Even so, it can't see very well. It has **antennae** on its head. They help it find its way around.

WOW!

Some kinds of caterpillars have prickly spines. They can be poisonous.

Growing Bigger

Caterpillars have one main job: eating!
The young caterpillar eats leaves.
It starts with the leaf it hatched on.
It eats almost all the time.

The caterpillar grows quickly.
Soon it is too big for its skin.
The old skin splits. There
is new skin underneath.
The caterpillar wiggles out.
This is called **molting**.

The caterpillar molts
after about three days.
Its new skin has yellow
and black stripes.

The Chrysalis

The caterpillar molts five times. Before the last molt, it hangs from a leaf or branch. Its skin slowly splits. Inside is a green covering.

The covering is called a **chrysalis**. The caterpillar stays inside for a week or two. Its body is changing. It is becoming an adult. It is turning into a butterfly.

A monarch chrysalis is pale green.

Beautiful Wings

Finally, the **chrysalis** splits. The butterfly pushes its way out. Its body still has three main parts. But it doesn't look like a caterpillar anymore. It now has wings.

The wings are tightly folded to fit inside the chrysalis.

The wings are orange and black. At first, they are wet and wrinkled. The butterfly spreads them out. Soon they dry. The butterfly is ready to fly for the first time.

Taking Flight

Most monarch butterflies live for a few weeks. The ones that come out in late summer live longer. They make a long journey. They fly south to escape the winter cold.

Staying close together helps the butterflies keep warm.

WOW!

Ladybugs and some wasps rest through the winter, too.

Most of the butterflies fly to Mexico. They find forests of fir trees. Thousands of butterflies **roost** in each tree. They rest until spring.

Starting Again

In spring, it gets warmer. The butterflies begin their trip home. They don't get very far. They **mate** and lay eggs. Then they die.

Each butterfly only makes part of the journey.

The life cycle is starting again. The eggs hatch. The caterpillars turn into butterflies. They continue their journey. It is thousands of miles long.

The Life Cycle

A butterfly lays an egg on a leaf.

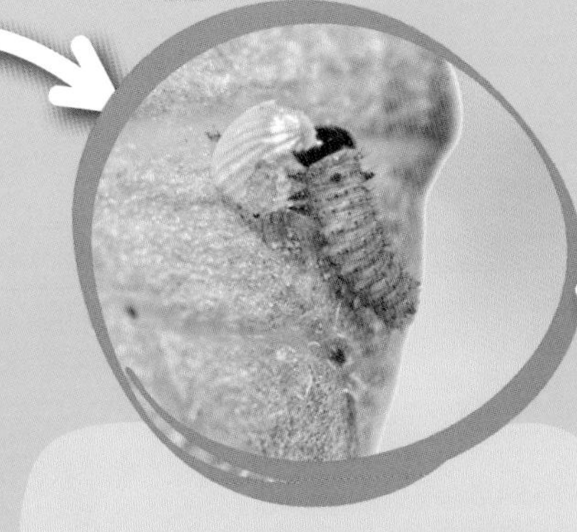

A caterpillar hatches from the egg.

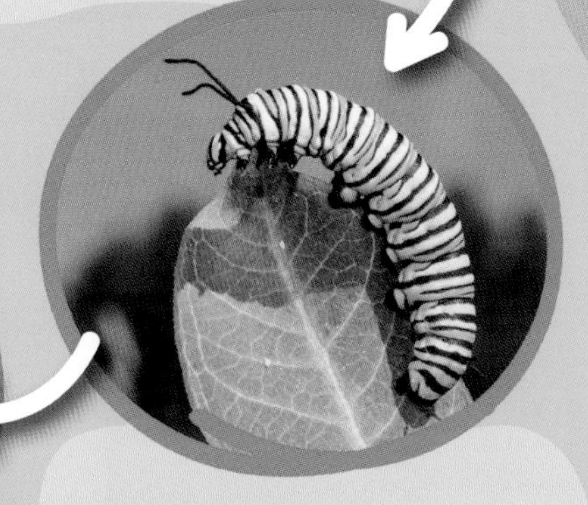

The caterpillar grows and changes.

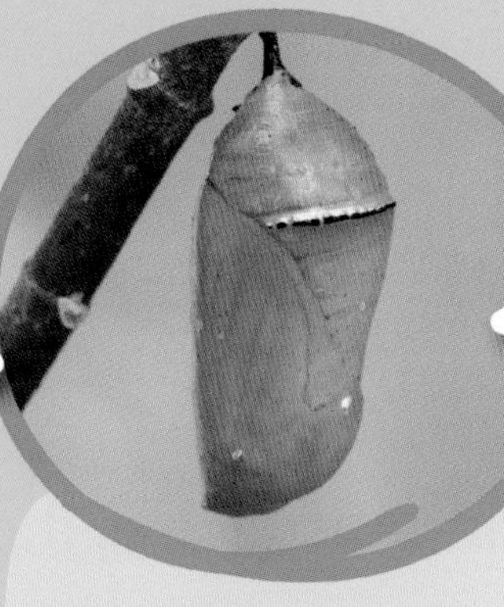

The caterpillar forms a chrysalis.

A butterfly comes out of the chrysalis.

Fact File

Overall life span: about 7 weeks to about 10 months

Caterpillar size: 0.25 to 1.75 inches (0.6 to 4 cm)

Butterfly wingspan: 3 to 4 inches (8 to 10 cm)

Diet: caterpillars eat leaves; butterflies sip nectar from flowers

WOW!

A butterfly's long tongue is hollow like a straw, for sucking up nectar.

Try It!

Research the migration of monarch butterflies. Mark their journey on a map of North America.

Can you find other types of butterflies that also migrate? How far do these butterflies travel?

Other types of animals migrate, too. Humpback whales, leatherback sea turtles, wildebeest, and robins all migrate. How do their journeys compare?

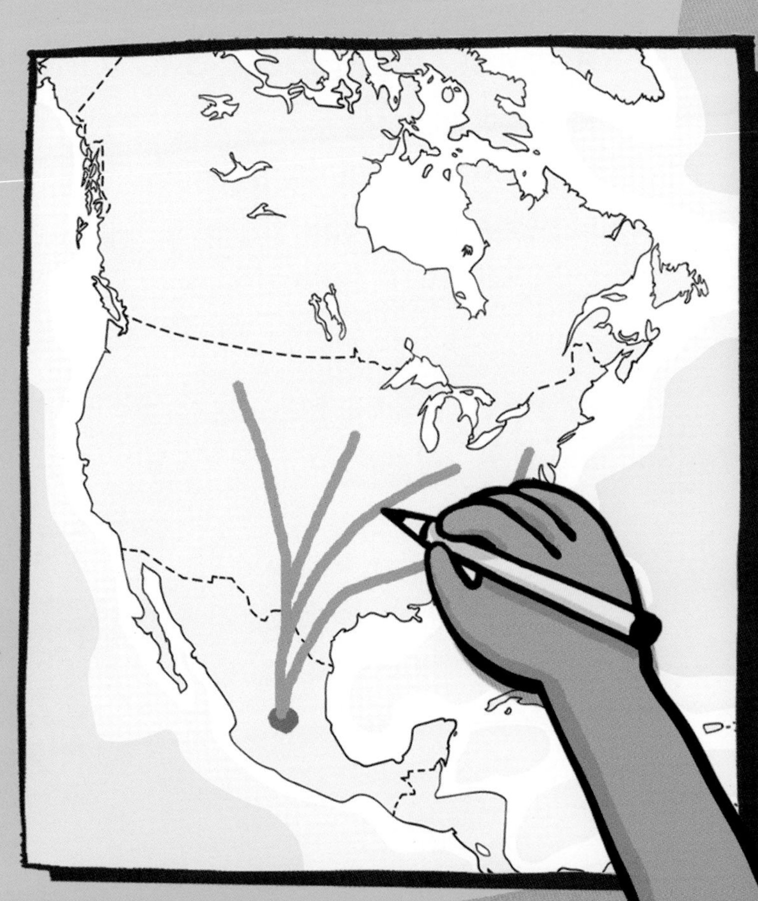

Useful Words

antennae a pair of long, thin feelers on the heads of most insects and some other animals

chrysalis a protective covering for a caterpillar as it is turning into an adult

disguise a way of changing your appearance in order to hide

larva the young stage of many insects' life cycle. A caterpillar is the larva of a butterfly.

mate to come together with another animal to make babies

molting shedding a skin that is too small to reveal a new one underneath

roost to rest or sleep

Find out More

Websites

www.dkfindout.com/uk/animals-and-nature/insects/butterfly-life-cycle/

www.fs.fed.us/wildflowers/pollinators/Monarch_Butterfly/migration/index.shtml

monarchlab.org/biology-and-research/biology-and-natural-history/breeding-life-cycle/

Books

A Butterfly's Life Cycle Mary R. Dunn, Capstone 2017

We Travel So Far Laura Knowles, Words & Pictures 2017

When Butterflies Cross the Sky: The Monarch Butterfly Migration Sharon Katz Cooper, Picture Window Books 2015

Index